**Rejoice in the Lord always: and again I say, Rejoice. Philippians 4:4.**

I remember being quite depressed some days, weeks and months throughout my life, feeling low in my spirit. People would say just "Rejoice in the Lord!" or "Be happy!" You know all the encouraging phrases that are so easily said within the church going crowd. During these dark times, I wanted to say "that is easy for you but I can't do it". During these dark times, I wanted to say "maybe that is easy for you but I can't do it." Sometimes their words would actually make me angry.

As time went on, and as I drew near to God continually, He drew near to me continually, and things eventually got better. The bible says, **"Draw near To God, and he will draw near to you." James 4:8.** I still can't rejoice in the Lord always, but it is getting a whole lot easier and I rejoice in Him much more often. The actual definitions of the word rejoice means to feel joyful; and be delighted. So, if you have been feeling down today I want encourage you to at least try to be delighted in your salvation.

Through all my experiences that I have had with depression, I've learned a few things along the way. One of which, is that I am naturally empathetic towards depressed people; most times, I can sense and feel some of their emotional pain. This helps me to help others. I learned not tell people just to be happy, but rather to share with them and try to assist them on getting to where they need to be spiritually. I will also explain my situation to them and empathize with theirs.

So, remember today that God can use the bad times for good. **And we know that all things work together for good to them that love God, to them who are the called according to his purpose. Romans 8: 28.**

**A merry heart doeth good like a medicine: but a broken spirit drieth the bones. Proverbs 17:22**

Did you know that laughter triggers the release of endorphins in our body? Endorphins are the body's own natural painkillers. In addition, laughter produces a general sense of well-being. These endorphins also assist your immune system, which is obviously very important. Over the years, there has been a lot of research done on this topic and yet the bible has had this nugget of information for years. You can actually laugh your way to health. I remember reading a story about a man who was dying of cancer; I believe that he was told his chances were slim on surviving. He decided to give up the treatment and on the doctors all together and just go home. On his way, home he picked up a large assortment of movies, all of which were comedies. He got into his bed and watched them one after another. He laughed, laughed, and watched one right after the other and continued laughing. To the doctor's amazement this man's cancer was gone, all healed. It's an amazing story right?

I've often thought people who had health issues that are connected to bone fractures or sore bones, and I sometimes wonder if their spirit was broken for a very long period of time. The bible tells us that Jesus came to heal, **"He heals the brokenhearted and binds up their wounds." Psalm 147:3**

God want us to be joyful. Sometimes this can be very hard for individuals especially if they suffer from depression. Sometimes, nothing even seems funny or there is nothing happening that makes you to want to remotely crack a smile. You might even resort to the fake smile just to get people off your back. I've done that when I was down.

Spiritual Prescription: Listen to praise music all day, even if you don't feel like it. If you don't have any, try to get some from someone. The bible says to **"Put on the Garment of Praise for the Spirit of Heaviness" Isaiah 61:3**. Thank God for all your blessings even if they even if they seem small or basic. Write them down in a journal. **"Give thanks in all circumstances for this is God's will." Thessalonians 5:18.**

**"Thy word is a lamp unto my feet, and a light unto my path."
Psalm 119:105**

Imagine walking down a bumpy, winding road in the middle of the night without any light except maybe the odd firefly that beams by. It would be very scary, right? Moreover, you probably would trip on a tree stump or a huge rock sticking out of the gravel road or you might fall and scrape your knees. Well, it seems that life without God is much like that scenario. Scared, falling lost, without any direction.  Thank God, we have him in those times and thank God, we can have him to talk to every day.

I think of all the huge strides mankind has made and how far technology has advanced, with wireless Internet and blue tooth, it goes on and on.  Just think we have wireless access to God the Father anytime. No contract, no fees, no breaking of a device or charging it. He is always there to listen to our every need; he cares for us and will never leave us.

**I will never leave thee nor forsake thee. Hebrews 13:5**

*Day 4*

**Finally, my brethren, be strong in the Lord, and in the power of his might. Put on the whole armor of God that ye may be able to stand against the wiles of the devil. For we wrestle not against flesh and blood, but against principalities, against powers, against the rulers of the darkness of this world, against spiritual wickedness in high places. Wherefore take unto you the whole armor of God, that ye may be able to withstand in righteousness; And your feet shod with the preparation of the gospel of peace; Above all, taking the shield of faith, wherewith ye shall be able to quench all the fiery darts of the wicked. And take the helmet of salvation, and the sword of the Spirit, which is the word of God: Praying always with all prayer and supplication in the Spirit, and watching thereunto withal perseverance and supplication for all saints; Ephesians 6:10-18**

Picture a soldier getting ready for war, but this one particular day he decides to not wear any protective gear. Maybe he thinks it will take too long to put on. Today this soldier just wears pair of old jeans and a t-shirt. He just walks out into the battlefield and expects to live the same as other days, victorious.

In the same sense, as believers if we don't put on all that we need, all the armor on a daily basis in our Christian walk it can be extremely hard to stand against evil. The bible says we need to put on the whole armor to stand against the wiles of the devil.

Definition of the word wiles: 1) a stratagem or trick intended to deceive or ensnare. 2) A disarming or seductive manner, device, or procedure: the wiles of a skilled negotiator. 3) Trickery; cunning.

Doesn't that definition sound just like Satan? Be careful today and protect yourself from the devil's lies and trickery. Don't believe his lies that might say, "You will always suffer from depression." Keep standing on the promises of God. Find promises in the bible put them up on your fridge, on your mirror and walls.

**Now faith is the substance of things hoped for, the evidence of things not seen. Hebrews 11:1**

Faith is hope that is not seen. Faith is the act of believing in something that you don't see. I heard about the planet Mars, I saw pictures but I was never there. Yet, I still believe there is a planet called Mars. We don't see God physically but we know that He is there. The same is true with the promises of the bible. Sometimes when you are quite depressed you might think, "God seems to answer other people's prayers but not mine." It can be an extremely difficult thing to do, trying to keep the faith and to keep on believing in the promises. Trust me when I say that it is more difficult not to believe in the promises of God.

**So, then faith cometh by hearing, and hearing by the word of God. Romans 10:17** I love this verse because it has been true to my life. Many times my faith seemed weak and I felt like I needed to have my faith increased. I listened to the bible in an audio version and this helped immensely. It took time to sink into my spiritual pores but it helped very much. Faith cometh by hearing… I believe the same is true of doubt. Doubt cometh by hearing, and hearing by doubtful people or beliefs. You often hear about some individuals who suffered from hearing much verbal abuse from parents or spouses, etc. Unfortunately, people start believing what they hear. "You're good for nothing," or "You are such a loser," you will never amount to anything." This type of behavior can affect people's lives in many negative forms. Some people won't even bother trying anything because that small voice of doubt rings loud in their head, "You will fail."

Replace the doubtful and hurting phrases with scriptures of faith. Memorize them and keep them near to your heart. The more you hear the word of God the more it will dwell in your soul. It can heal and cast out doubt. If you need more faith, today I encourage you to read or even listen to an audio version of the bible. God will bless you and lift your spirits. And the scripture, **foreseeing that God would justify the ... Jesus came to destroy the works of the devil and set the captives free ... Galatians 3:8-9.** Don't be a slave anymore.

**Casting down imaginations, and every high thing that exalteth itself against the knowledge of God, and bringing into captivity every thought to the obedience of Christ; 2 Corinthians 10:5.**

Training our mind and bringing every thought to the obedience of Christ is not an easy task, but it is attainable. First, it takes a person to be aware of the situation; secondly, it takes a wholehearted commitment. Lastly, it takes perseverance and determination. Change the way your mind thinks. When you get a negative thought, have another positive thought ready to immediately replace it. Say that you are struggling with jealousy or envy; first look up some verses in the bible and write them down concerning the subject. Memorize at least 2-3 verses, now this is what you will be filling that slot with. Eventually, you will not be struggling with it, and it will return less and less times. Practice these tips for that nasty imagination. We all have struggled with it. It is best to get it in the beginning stages, but it is never too late.

**The prayer of a righteous man is powerful and effective. James 5:16.**

This verse used to make me sometimes think that my prayers weren't answered because I wasn't righteous enough. However, the truth of the matter is we all have sinned and praying or the act of prayer is a way of being on the way to the path of righteousness. I like to pray throughout the day, pray without ceasing or stopping. I pray when I am driving, (I never close my eyes while driving). Ha Ha.

While I am sure, you get the idea. Another way I pray is I have a prayer journal. I pray, Dear God, or Dear Heavenly Father, It is so interesting to look back and see the answered prayer and the ones that I am still waiting on. I encourage you to make some habits throughout your day that include prayer. Talk to Jesus he wants to be your friend.

*Dear God, I pray for the depressed and the oppressed, lift their spirits today. Make their heart anew; give them a new song of praise. In Jesus, name Amen.*

**Blessed is the man that walketh not in the counsel of the ungodly, nor standeth in the way of sinners, nor sitteth in the seat of the scornful. But his delight is in the law of the LORD; and in his law doth he meditate day and night. And he shall be like a tree planted by the rivers of water, that bringeth forth his fruit in his season; his leaf also shall not wither; and whatsoever he doeth shall prosper. Psalm 1:1-3.**

Today it seems that every second person that I talked to is into yoga, or meditation. I'm not saying these things are necessarily bad for you but it is much more beneficial to meditate on the Word of God. The definitions of the word meditate: Meditate means to reflect on; contemplate. To plan in the mind; intend: Trees that are planted by water grow roots that are so deep that a hurricane couldn't pull them down. Don't you want to be like that with your faith? I do. So strong, that nothing that life throws at you will take you down. Meditate on the word of God and you shall be like that tree planted by the water. **My eyes stay open through the watches of the night that I may meditate on your promises. Psalms 119:148.** Praise God for the Psalms.

"But now, O Lord, You are our Father; we are the clay, and You our potter; and all we are the work of Your hand." Isaiah 64:8

For, we are God's masterpiece. He has created us anew in Christ Jesus, so we can do the good things he planned for us long ago. Ephesians 2:10.

Imagine us being one clump of clay without mold or form. God wants to mold us. Let God mold you because he is the potter and He will make you into what he wants you to be. He has a plan for your life. The bible says that he planned things for us long ago. You are his masterpiece.

**And forgive us our sins, as we have forgiven those who sin against us. Matthew 6:12**

Forgiveness can be an extremely hard thing to do, but holding bitterness in our heart is actually harder.  It is also is detrimental to your health. Can you think of anyone that you haven't forgiven? We read in the bible about forgiving others, we know it is right. There has been numerous scientific studies done on forgiveness and it has been known to beneficial to our health.  It makes sense. When you are angry or have a grudge, your food doesn't digest properly; you may eat faster and not even chew properly. You might even make bad choices of what to eat because of stress; you probably would eat more fast food. Because of not forgiving someone you might not play anymore or hardly ever, thus causing more stress. Bitterness can grow in your heart and affect your immune system. If you think that forgiving someone is a hard task, I assure you that it is harder not to forgive him or her. You might say, "You don't know what they did to me or said to me," no, I don't, but God does, and he will help you overcome and forgive. We hear all this talk about forgiveness and usually it is about forgiving others. We also need to remember to forgive ourselves. Shame, guilt, and anger can be causes to depression. Forgive yourself today as well.

**A double minded man is unstable in all his ways. James 1:8**

Have you ever met anyone who acts one way then another way around Christians?  Maybe we have all done this at one time or another. Fortunately, I have learned to be myself around pretty much everyone. One time I was cutting a church member's hair from a church I once attended. I cut hair as a hobby for family and friends. To my surprise, she said that she found they way I talked refreshing. Often times Christians think that they should act or say only certain things or tip toe around various topics. Meanwhile, God knows our hearts and he uses other believers to help us. Therefore, I am honest.

Although, I still feel that sometimes I am double minded and God needs to work in my heart. Suffering from depression isn't easy and we shouldn't really be too hard on ourselves.

**Being confident of this very thing, that he which hath begun a good work in you will perform it until the day of Jesus Christ. Philippians 1:6**

*Day 12*

**But grow in grace, and in the knowledge of our Lord and Savior Jesus Christ. To him be glory both now and forever. Amen. 2 Peter 3:18.**

We all know that growing plants requires some tender care and some work. Watering and sunshine are essential. Some people seem to have that green thumb and plants grow for them easily. Nevertheless, they probably just learned the secrets and practiced them. The same is true for the Christian. God wants us to grow spiritually and for a good reason. It takes some work as well. He wants to prepare us for Glory. Satan doesn't want us to grow. He wants our faith to die off. He doesn't want us to branch out in our faith. He will try many different things to get us distracted from growing. Therefore, we need to remember to be on guard. Be on guard today.

**Guard your heart, for it is the wellspring of life. Proverbs 4:23.**

*Day 13*

**Finally, brethren, whatsoever things are true, whatsoever things are honest, whatsoever things are just, whatsoever things are pure, whatsoever things are lovely, whatsoever things are of good report; if there be any virtue, and if there be any praise, think on these things. Philippians 4:8**

Have you ever thought that perhaps you will never be healed from depression? I have entertained this thought many times this before. The statement that I chose to believe was, "I will have depression my whole life." If you believe negative statements like this and keep re-affirming them every single day, then, yes it might be true. I have struggled with depression since the age of sixteen off and on. I've been on medication off and on for years. Medication did help me for a while. About five years ago, a doctor told me, "You need to be on medication (anti-depressants) your whole life." I made two attempts to go off them because of the side effects. The first time I needed to go back on and then the next time it was final. Did I get depressed again? Yes. However, I was able to cope with it thanks to depending on the Lord. This is where the difference lies. God gave me resources and strength to cope with it. Over time, I developed more and more coping skills or God gave me the skills.

**But my God shall supply all your need according to his riches in glory by Christ Jesus. Philippians 4:19.** If are on medication. Please don't go off them because of what you have read here. Instead, pray about it and seek counsel, get a few opinions etc. Take time to make this decision and talk to a doctor. The key to healing is faith. God wants to heal you.

**But he was wounded for our transgressions; he was bruised for our iniquities: the chastisement of our peace was upon him; and with his stripes we are healed. Isaiah 53:5.** Remember that God uses the bad in our lives for positive later on. **And we know that all things work together for good to them that love God, to them who are the called according to his purpose. Romans 8:28.**

**But the fruit of the Spirit is love, joy, peace, patience, kindness, goodness, faithfulness, gentleness, self-control; against such things there is no law. Galatians 5:22-23. Rejoice in the Lord always; again I will say, Rejoice. Philippians 4:4.**

Sometimes, life seems like it is full of pain. How can we have more joy? Reading the bible helps. Thinking on good thoughts and things help a lot. How we deal with pain is very important. Some people are self-destructive and end up making decisions that cause even more pain. I know that I have done this in the past. We are human and God knows that we are not perfect. He made us and He loves us. Here are some bible scriptures to ponder. I hope you like them.

**Joy comes after suffering, for his anger is but for a moment, and his favor is for a lifetime. Weeping may tarry for the night, but joy comes with the morning. Psalm 30:5.**

**A merry heart doeth good like a medicine: but a broken spirit drieth the bones. Proverbs 17:22**

**By prayer He prays to God and finds favor with him, he sees God's face and shouts for joy; he is restored by God to his righteous state. Job 33:26**

**By trusting him The LORD is my strength and my shield; my heart trusts in him, and I am helped. My heart leaps for joy and I will give thanks to him in song. Psalm 28:7**

**You will show me the path of life; in your presence is fullness of joy, at Your right hand there are pleasures forevermore. Psalm 16: 11.**

**Casting all your care upon him; for he careth for you. 1 Peter 5:7.**

Have you ever felt someone else's emotional pain so much that it made you burst into uncontrollable tears? This is what had happen to me. It was probably almost a year ago now. There was some plumbing done and some of the drywall that needed to be replaced in our apartment. Our caretaker told us that someone would be coming out to fix it soon and that they would be given keys to enter our suite.

The afternoon the man came, I was already at home. He seemed like a nice man. He was in his mid-fifties or early sixties. I sensed something from him, but at first, I wasn't sure what it was. We chatted about the apartment, agency, and the repairs. He said that he was sorry that he didn't come sooner to finish the work. He also mentioned that it because he had some family problems. At that time, I sensed that he didn't really want to talk about it. He just worked and chatted about everyday things. An hour went by and then my husband arrived home. They talked about the repairs and stuff of that nature too. The man then said he had to get some supplies from his truck and would that he would be back shortly. When he left I said to my husband, "something really bad happen and I think it has to do with children". He also sensed that maybe something bad happen to this man.

I suddenly felt a rush of emotional pain and burst out into tears. It was like I felt this man's pain for a few minutes. I wiped my tears just as he was coming back in the door. He then asked us if we wanted some concert tickets and the concert was this evening. We said sure and asked why he couldn't go. All he said was that he couldn't go and would like if we could use them. It was for that evening. We thanked him and invited him to stay and have coffee and a snack but he refused and said he would be right back. He came back with the tickets and again we thanked him. As he was leaving out the door he said, "I can't go because my daughter committed suicide last night," and he shut the door. We were shocked. I started crying again and went downstairs where he was. He had some of his supplies in the laundry room that was in the basement. I said, I'm so sorry please come back upstairs and talk. I told him to try to take time off. He explained that he had to keep moving and working. He said his daughter was thirty years old and had made two previous attempts. I believe he said she had two children. She suffered from depression and they sought help for her many times. He said he had to go. I gave this stranger a hug and through my tears muttered, "take care." I asked him to come back and visit sometime. That night we went to the concert and I didn't enjoy myself. I just kept thinking of the pain of the family and how the daughter might have been feeling. It was a very, very sad way to get free tickets. It is so unfortunate that this tragedy happened. I feel deeply for this family's pain. We have to be reminded to cast all our cares on Jesus. He feels our pain.

*Day 16*

**But he himself went a day's journey into the wilderness, and came and sat down under a juniper tree: and he requested for himself that he might die; and said, It is enough; now, O LORD, take away my life; for I am not better than my fathers. And as he lay and slept under a juniper tree, behold, then an angel touched him, and said unto him, arise and eat. And he looked, and, behold, there was a cake baken on the coals, and a cruse of**

**water at his head. And he did eat and drink, and laid him down again. And the angel of the LORD came again the second time, and touched him, and said, Arise and eat; because the journey is too great for thee. And he arose, and did eat and drink, and went in the strength of that meat forty days and forty nights unto Horeb the mount of God. 1 Kings 19: 4-8**

You are invited to a pity party. If you got an invitation like this, would you respond? So many people including myself have brought people down with their little pity parties. I remember I once had a Tupperware party and it was supposed to be a good time of ladies getting together. One lady from our church ruined the party with her troubles. I know I sound cold, but I always heard her complaints and they were always about her husband. In addition, I was a lot younger and somewhat less empathetic. (God has changed me a lot since then). Although that I may sound harsh, I do know what it is like when you are unhappy about something. In times like this, you want to seek help by talking about it. Unfortunately, she did bring down my little get together.

There is a time and place for everything. This lady's husband was not a bad guy; he had worked shift work and was tired most of the time. In addition, his hobby was recording Christian radio shows and he didn't pay that much attention to her or least give her the attention she wanted or needed. She just seemed so unhappy with the marriage and it was hard to listen to all the time. We have all been there at one time or another, frustrated, lonely and desperate for help or counsel.

I think of Elijah in the desert how he had his own little pity party. Actually, he seemed quite depressed. He even asked God to take away his life. I wonder what that cake was that made of that gave him strength for forty days. Maybe it was made with juniper berries. This would be the first angel food cake. We may not have an angel bake a cake for us but we can read the Word of God and pray to gather strength daily.

*Day 17*

**The Spirit of the Lord is upon me, because he hath anointed me to preach the gospel to the poor; he hath sent me to heal the brokenhearted, to preach deliverance to the captives, and recovering of sight to the blind, to set at liberty them that are bruised. Luke 4:18**

Captive- 1. One, such as a prisoner of war, who is forcibly confined, subjugated, or enslaved. 2. One held in the grip of a strong emotion or passion. Taken and held prisoner, as in war. 3. Held in bondage; enslaved. 4. Kept under restraint or control; confined: 4. Restrained by circumstances that prevent free choice:

Jesus came to set the captives free. We are living in a spiritual battlefield. If you feel like you have been taken as a prisoner then remember who is all powerful and came to set you free. The chains of bondage can be broken. The deep lies of Satan's deception can be broken. The strongholds can be loosed. You are a child of God. Claim your spot in the kingdom through Christ. There is freedom, don't give up in seeking the freedom that Christ offers.

*Heavenly Father, I pray for those that are struggling in the midst of spiritual warfare. I pray that you could give them freedom, victory and wisdom that they will need. In Jesus Name , Amen.*

Blessed are the poor in spirit, for theirs is the kingdom of heaven. Blessed are they who mourn, for they shall be comforted. Blessed are the meek, for they shall inherit the earth. Blessed are they who hunger and thirst for righteousness, for they shall be satisfied. Blessed are the merciful, for they shall obtain mercy. Blessed are the pure of heart, for they shall see God. Blessed are the peacemakers, for they shall be called children of God. Blessed are they who are persecuted for the sake of righteousness, for theirs is the kingdom of heaven." Matthew 5:3-10.

*Dear Heavenly Father, I pray that you can make us more like your son Jesus. I pray that we will remember to have mercy and be humble in spirit. Use our everyday lives to show others how to get to know you and help us to encourage broken spirits. I pray that others will come to know your gentle spirit. Fill us with your Holy Spirit and give us all the right attitude or beatitudes. In your precious name, I pray amen.*

*Day 19*

**We are fools for Christ's sake, but ye are wise in Christ; we are weak, but ye are strong; ye are honorable, but we are despised. 1 Corinthians 4:10.**

If you are feeling weak today, remember God uses the weak. If you are being foolish today, remember he uses the foolish. So, don't go into the self-condemning mode, instead just try to remember God created us with emotions and weaknesses. If he wanted perfect people, he would have probably just made robot like humans. In our weakness, he makes us strong somehow. Although we might not notice the strengths, he gives us until later on. An often believer are called weak or fools just for believing. May God show us our strengths through Christ today.

**God is our refuge and strength, a very present help in trouble. Therefore will not we fear, though the earth be removed, and though the mountains be carried into the midst of the sea; Though the waters thereof roar and be troubled, though the mountains shake with the swelling thereof. Psalm 46: 1-3**

.

A few months ago, I went through a very long hard trial. In the beginning when it first happened immediately the Holy Spirit spoke to my spirit and said, "Everything is going to be OK." I actually had a peace about it all and trusted the Lord. Unfortunately, as the weeks and months went by I let doubt creep in. Slowly but surely, it had a foothold in my spirit that caused pure havoc in my spirit and mind. I worried and spent an excessive amount of time thinking about it. In-between my bouts of worry and doubt I continued praying. What caused the doubt? I was listening to people and their ideas, or negative thoughts. Allowing myself to believe their doubts and fears, I began to say to myself, "maybe it was just me and not the spirit." Satan is at the root of all doubt and is the one who is mostly responsible for it. Nevertheless, we make our own choices of what and whom we are going to believe.

Now that everything is actually OK, I know that God taught me not to waver and not to sink through any trial, but rather to just to keep on trusting in Him, for He is faithful always. Doubt takes away from your faith. Doubt can seep in like water in a leaky boat and eventually sink you. We must patch up the holes with faith to stay afloat.

*Dear Heavenly Father, I pray for anyone on the who might be going through a trial right now, I pray that you will fill them with joy and a peace that passeth all understanding. In Jesus' Name I pray, Amen.*

**"Come to Me, all you who labor and are heavy laden, and I will give you rest. Take My yoke upon you and learn from Me, for I am gentle and lowly in heart, and you will find rest for your souls. For My yoke is easy and My burden is light." Matthew 11:28-30.**

I remember when I was a new Christian. I would look on outward appearances and I would judge people on things that they wearing or things that they did. Later, through difficult times and circumstances I took my eyes off the Lord and backslid from my faith. I then had people judge me, mostly Christians. Therefore, I knew and know what it feels like. I now think they that we need to more gentle. The Holy Spirit is the one that convicts the heart. Yes, the word of God is sharper than any two-edge sword but the spirit is gentle. Sometimes we forget the journey and are too zealous to let God work things out in people's lives. Remember God uses your past experiences for good. **And we know that all things work together for good to them that love God, to them who are the called according to his purpose. Romans 8:28**

Let us pray for one another.

**IIe that committeth sin is of the devil; for the devil sinneth from the beginning. For this purpose the Son of God was manifested, that he might destroy the works of the devil. 1 John 3:8.**

When I was about sixteen or seventeen years old, I had experimented with the occult realm. Even though I had went to Sunday school as a child and learned about the gospel, I had stopped seeking God and began to seek the other side, the dark side. I'm sure because of dabbling in the occult strange things started happening to me.

One night, I was up all night with insomnia and racing thoughts, I smelled this smell. It smelled like sulfur. I quickly cleaned my bedroom, emptied the garbage, ashtrays and so forth but the smell continued to linger. There was also a heavy evil presence mingled with the horrible stench. I was terrified and gripped with fear. I grabbed the bible that I had won at Sunday school for memorizing bible verses. I started reading it and the presence along with its smell went away. Not long after, I eventually sought the Lord and renounced all the dealings with the occult.

A few years later, I was reading a Christian book (I can't remember the name) but the author mentioned that they had had a similar experience. He said that the sulfur smell was the smells of hell! And that we should rebuke it in the Name of Jesus! Jesus is the word.

Have you ever had any dark side supernatural experiences? Moreover, did you know that Jesus spoke more about hell than heaven? If you have ever dabbled in the occult, Tarot cards or Ouija boards, then I encourage you to renounce these things today. Pray and name the association you had with the occult and ask for forgiveness. Also, pray that God will take away any spirits that are attached to these things, pray for them to be gone. The words renounce means to give up especially by a formal announcement.

**Why are you downcast, O my soul? Why so disturbed within me? Put your hope in God, for I will yet praise him, my Savior and my God. Psalm 43:5.**

One day, I was feeling real down.  After I wrote a bunch of yucky emotions in my journal, and I felt a bit better. I was back on the right track. Sometimes expressing your moodiness in a creative format is much better than taking it out on yourself or others. Change the gear of your mood by praising God. You might think, "Well, I don't feel like praising God."  Or "I'm too depressed to praise God. Just try it anyway and see what happens.

**But as for me, I will always have hope; I will praise you more and more. Psalm 71:14**.  We must keep pressing on when we get down and discouraged.  Besides what other choice do we have? This is the best choice. Here are some steps to help you along your way. Pray for strength to do it.  If you can't pray because you are too distraught then ask others to pray for you. Prayer is powerful. Get your mind off yourself and think about others, help others and pray for others. Sing some songs of praises or just listen to some encouraging music, even if you don't feel like it. Try it.

**And said, If thou wilt diligently hearken to the voice of the LORD thy God, and wilt do that which is right in his sight, and wilt give ear to his commandments, and keep all his statutes, I will put none of these diseases upon thee, which I have brought upon the Egyptians: for I am the LORD that healeth thee. Ezekiel 15:26**

Hearken means- to listen attentively; give heed.

Diligent means- marked by persevering, painstaking effort

I remember being taught that Egypt was known as the world or worldly. I learned this at a bible study. My sister was diagnosed with stage 3 colon cancer, she had it removed but still had to undergo Chemotherapy. She is doing quite well considering. She is still working at her government job and she is presently involved in the dating scene. She has some bad days but overall I think she is doing great. I've been praying for her. She has one treatment left. I think she is brave even though I know that she is scared to death. She is not a Christian as far as I know. I want to ask all the believers that read this if they could pray for her, for salvation and healing. Thank you so much.

We all need to hearken to the Lord and some of us need healing more than others. If we are already close to the Lord or seeking him daily it will be much easier. Let us try to seek Him diligently.

Day 25

**For my thoughts are not your thoughts, neither are your ways my ways, saith the LORD. For as the heavens are higher than the earth, so are my ways higher than your ways, and my thoughts than your thoughts. Isaiah 55:8-9.**

We often hear this saying, "God works in mysterious ways," even though this phrase is actually not a bible verse there are some scriptures that support the saying. The above scripture is one of them. Sometimes we think we know what God should do or exactly how He should answer our prayers.

Nevertheless, most times God works in mysterious ways. God will place us at certain locations of employment or in certain situations. Maybe God uses our vehicles breaking down and you riding the bus to meet someone. God uses other human beings to help us all the time. They don't even have to have the same faith as you and they don't even have to have the same lifestyle. God knows what we need and exactly where we are in our walk with him. In the past when I needed to talk to someone God has used people such as co-workers or family, even strangers to help me. This happened to me many, many times. I'm sure that I have helped other people as well.

*Day 26*

**Blessed are the meek: for they shall inherit the earth. Matthew 5:5**

Who makes the standard for normal? A few years back I had worked with adults who had special needs, (learning, physical and mental disabilities). I learned a lot about life from these individuals. We all do and say different things that maybe interpreted among some circles of people that might not be considered normal. The people that I worked with have such a loving personality and are so accepting it melted my heart. It amazes me how that in our society or rather according to society that these people are the ones who are labeled not normal. Yet, when we are rude to each other or impatient while driving etc, etc, we are still deemed normal. When you suffer from depression, sometimes you might feel like you don't quite fit in this world. Just remember that God loves you and wants to work in your heart and life. These individuals were truly meek and God wants to make us meek as well.

**A glad heart makes a cheerful countenance, but by sorrow of heart the spirit is broken. The mind of him who has understanding, seeks knowledge, inquires after and craves it, but the mouths of (self-confident) fools feed on folly. Proverbs 15:13-14.**

Grieving can last a long time. It's been almost six years now since my Grandma died. She had raised and I called her mom. There is not a day that goes by that I don't think about her or talk about her. I miss her so much. Near the end of her life, I was also going through some difficult things and it seemed as though I was almost angry with her for being sick. It was selfish of me. I think I was also grieving then. I didn't know how to deal with it. Therefore, because of it I have a lot of guilt mingled with a deep love and respect for her.

Grief is a funny thing even when you think you are done grieving, it hits you again. How you play things over and over again in your head about if you could only be with her again. How I would act or what I would say. We always think and ask ourselves, "Did they know how much I loved them." We all express our love and fears different and we all grieve differently. I think because of it we make different decisions in our lives. Sometimes, decisions are made from pain and they are not always the right decisions. On the other hand, sometimes we make decisions on what are loved ones would have liked if they were here. This is all part of grieving. I think that it is normal to think about them and cry at times.

Crying is one of my healing tools. It cleanses and can be a good release. I think that our loved ones knew how much we loved them and of course, they would want us to be happy because that's what people want for you when they love you. Grief can be another reason or cause for depression.  If you are grieving from the loss of a loved one, divorce or another kind of life's tragedies, I encourage you today to seek counsel. The bible says a wise person seeks counsel.

**Even the youths shall faint and be weary, and the young men shall utterly fall: But they that wait upon the LORD shall renew their strength; they shall mount up with wings as eagles; they shall run, and not be weary; and they shall walk, and not faint. Isaiah 40:31**

Sometimes when we are waiting for an answered prayer, we become weary. We become tired and begin to doubt. The bible says that if we wait upon God that He will renew our strength. I believe He will renew our faith as well. In a world with instantaneous products and all the technology, we sometimes expect our prayers answers instantly too. We as a society are not used of waiting for anything. Wait upon God today for your strength.

**Confess your faults one to another, and pray one for another, that ye may be healed. The effectual fervent prayer of a righteous man availeth much. James 5:16.**

Did you know the bible actually tells us to confess your sins to one another? In addition, it says to pray for one another. If you don't have, close Christian friends try to find someone either at your church or a Christian organization (even online). You could also pray about finding a close friend like this. Confess your faults to each other in confidence of course. This is extremely beneficial and has many great healing benefits. Jesus is our best friend, but we must remember that He uses others. He also uses us in these ways too. Most pastors also provide free counseling. Check it out, don't hesitate this is just another step to healing.

**If any of you lack wisdom, let him ask of God, that giveth to all men liberally, and upbraideth not; and it shall be given him. James 1:5**

I encourage you to ask for wisdom because God gives it freely to us. Ask for wisdom concerning decisions that you make in everyday life. Wisdom is crucial in this world. We need it. Remember the Sunday school song "The wise man built his house upon the rock" Jesus is the rock and the rest is sinking sand. Ask God to give you wisdom concerning your depression and how to cope better with it. Our God is an amazing God and there is nothing that He can't do. Nothing! Solomon who was the wisest man in the bible, had the opportunity to ask God for anything at all, but he chose wisdom.

**Seek the Kingdom of God above all else, and he will give you everything you need. Luke 12:31**

*The End*

More by C.L. Griffin:

*Spiritual Food Daily Devotions*

*Devotions for the Anxious*

*Walking by Faith Devotions*

*A Pocket Full of Poems*

*Practical Daily Devotions*

*The Believer's Journey Collection of Poetry*

*Spirit Renewal Daily Devotions*

*Simple Grace Poems*

*Keep up the Faith Daily Devotions*

*Devotions for Couples Daily Devotions*

*Freedom for Christians with Addictions Daily Devotions*

Made in the USA
Lexington, KY
11 August 2015